A RIVER THAT
FLOWS TWO WAYS

THE HUDSON

CARR CLIFTON

FOREWORD BY JOHN MYLOD

WESTCLIFFE PUBLISHERS, INC. ENGLEWOOD, COLORADO

CONTENTS

International Standard Book Number:
  ISBN 0-929969-06-5
Library of Congress Catalogue Card Number:
  89-050274
Copyright, Photographs and Text: Carr Clifton, 1989.
  All rights reserved.
Editor: John Fielder
Assistant Editors: Margaret Terrell Morse, Elisa Adler
Production Manager: Mary Jo Lawrence
Typographer: Richard M. Kohen
Printed in Japan by Dai Nippon Printing Co., Ltd., Tokyo
Published by Westcliffe Publishers, Inc.
  2650 South Zuni Street, Englewood, Colorado 80110
No portion of this book, either photographs or text, may be
  reproduced in any form without the written permission of
  the publisher.

Bibliography

Bryant, William Cullen. *An Anthology of the New England Poets from Colonial Times to the Present Day.* New York: Random House, 1948.
John Burroughs' America, ed. Farida A. Wiley. Reprinted by permission of Devin-Adair Publishers, Greenwich, Connecticut. Copyright 1951.
Cooper, James Fenimore. *Last of the Mohicans.* New York: Bantam Publishers. Reprinted with permission.
Drake, Joseph Rodman. *The Culprit Fay.* New York: Carleton, 1867.
Irving, Washington. *The Writing of Washington Irving.* New York: Modern Library.
Rexroth, Kenneth. *Selected Poems.* New York: New Directions Publishing Corporation, 1984. Reprinted with permission.
Whitman, Walt. *Leaves of Grass (Comprising all of the poems written by Walt Whitman following the arrangement of the edition of 1891-2).* New York: Modern Library.

Westcliffe Publishers gratefully acknowledges Hitachi America, Ltd., without whose generous support this book would not have been possible.

Page 1: Columbine along the Hudson River
Page 2: Autumn in the Shawangunk Mountains, Minnewaska State Park
Page 3: Fall colors reflected in the Hudson River near Tahawus, Adirondack Park and Preserve
Right: Weathered gravestones at the Old Dutch Reformed Church, circa 1690s, North Tarrytown

JOHN MYLOD

FOREWORD

Out of the Adirondack wilderness, rushing forth from rocky brooks, tumbling over bread loaf boulders and running as a trout stream, the Hudson River levels out as it broadens, slows with the flood thrust of the ocean tide and, in turn, flows seaward to enrich the coastal zone with an amazing abundance of aquatic life.

The Hudson River is one of the wonders of the world. Its history is the story of America. This extraordinary waterway reflects images of the natural history and historic connections that combine in the country's social, scientific, cultural and aesthetic development. It serves as a storehouse for our heritage and a place where the romance of the past gives way to the encroaching reality of the here and now. Cooper's Natty Bumppo called it "all creation," and long before that, long before European settlers set foot in its valley, there were people partaking of the Hudson's bounty who had been drawn by prophesy and legend to the "river that flows two ways."

From the quiet of Lake Tear of the Clouds, one of the river's many sources, in mountains protected as "forever wild" by the state constitution, to the coastal bight beyond New York City's deep water harbor, the Hudson is relatively short as important rivers go — less than 325 miles in length — but its watershed reaches into five states and is home to nearly 10 percent of the nation's population. Within these boundaries is a seemingly limitless array of opportunities for exploration and delight. As a place with dramatic scenery, open space protection, historic preservation, recreation and a rich profusion of flora and fauna, the Hudson River Valley includes all of the attributes of a national park except the designation. But this is only part of the paradox.

For fully half its length the Hudson is actually an arm of the sea, an estuary, a river that flows two ways. Its physical, chemical and biological characteristics are combined in a complex mix of great beauty, diversity and productivity. In the estuary, sea water is diluted by fresh water from the land, and the blend determines how plants and animals will survive and grow in waters more productive than the richest soils on earth. As with other estuarine systems, the Hudson's chief biological function is to serve as a nursery so that young fish can develop in an environment that is protected and brimming with nourishment.

More than 190 species of fish rely on the Hudson as a spawning and nursery habitat. The estuary alone contributes more than 50 percent of the East Coast's striped bass stocks and is host to such fish commonly found in its waters as shad, stripers, 300-pound sturgeon, blue crab, anchovies, eel, tomcod, catfish, hogchokers and flounder. Oysters and clams were also once common in the lower estuary, until their seedbeds were destroyed by dredge and fill projects that scoured the river bottom for sand and gravel.

For centuries the river has been a magnet, drawing people to its shores to discover the mystery and magic of its resources. People see the Hudson as a drinking water supply, a deep water ship channel, a sewage disposal pipe, a community recreation resource, an industrial outfall stream, a commercial fishery, a tourist attraction and a guidebook to American history. Special pilots guide its largest ships to upriver landings, young oarsmen and women in racing shells pull against the tides, while in the lower estuary, watermen anchor their nets each spring in the Tappan Zee or, upriver, drift with the current to catch shad.

Along the shoreline bald eagles and ospreys soar above the traprock crags of the Palisades or nest in protected marshes of the National Estuarine Santuary system. Other eagles, including one of the largest wintering populations in the Northeast, prefer the wilderness ridges and clean-water lakes of the southern Catskills.

In the last century the landscapes of the Catskill and Shawangunk mountains also became the backdrops for the country's first school of painting, the Hudson River school. Along with the flow of trade and travel evolved the river's own special boat, the Hudson River sloop. For sport, hard water sailors developed iceboats that could outrun early steam trains and travel 60, 70, 80 miles an hour, which, at the time, was faster than anything else in the world of transportation.

Autumn leaves in potholes, Hudson River, Adirondack Park and Preserve

With the expansion of the railroad along the water level of the estuary during the last century, the river's shoreline changed dramatically. Construction of the right-of-way destroyed important habitat while at the same time significantly limiting public access to river resources. In the process, expansion of private development was also limited by the inability to get to the river at many locations. Inadvertently, the railroad contributed to a kind of land use protection and, along with rugged terrain and large tracts of privately held property, contributed to the preservation of aesthetically or ecologically important places.

By altering the shoreline the railroad cut off thousands of acres of shallow embayments from the river, but also adapted causeways to permit tidal flow to and from significant wetland areas such as Constitution Marsh and the Tivoli Bays. Dozens of smaller coves and wetlands behind the roadbed are also flushed daily by tidal action and contribute important food supplies to the main-stem river.

Back bay shallows and marshes are crucial to the productivity of the Hudson's complex estuarine ecosystem. These marshes filter and cleanse the waters. They serve as buffers between upland woodlots and the churning tides. They provide important habitats for killifish and kingfishers, muskrats and raccoons. Great blue herons and great horned owls live here. So do long-legged rails and snapping turtles. Here, too, are gardens of rooted grasses, wild rice and sweet flag.

But many of the river valley's important places — marshes, shallows, woodlands and historic resources — are vulnerable to the increase in development pressure that is being felt throughout the watershed. Ironically, as the environmental quality of the river system improves, the value of scenic and recreational resources skyrockets and thus threatens many productive areas. Commercial and residential growth has a direct impact on the Hudson, its large estates, its waterfront property, its tiny hamlets, its wetlands and its ridge lines. And yet, in the midst of urban and suburban sprawl along the Hudson, there are areas of wild and scenic beauty. There are grand vistas of dramatic proportions, as well as smaller slices of view corridors that inspire, bewitch and beguile.

Coupled with the pressure for change is a strong constituency for the protection of the river's resources. Over the past quarter century people have rallied to save a mountain, marshland, farmland, the river's historic places and the structures people believe are important touchstones with the past. Out of struggle and controversy have come science and conservation.

We now know much more about the river's role in the watershed and its important contributions to the productivity of coastal waters. Fishery research demonstrates that the Hudson's influence stretches from Nova Scotia to the Carolinas, but there remains a constant challenge to protect habitat and other river resources from efforts to develop the shoreline or to withdraw large amounts of water. Although the river is alive, its unrestricted use is curtailed by pollution problems that limit consumption as well as economic opportunity. Now, however, there is a growing realization that the health of the region is tied to the health of the river. Legislation has been passed and new management ideals expressed. Only the Hudson's future is at stake.

In the meantime, opportunities are everywhere to investigate the wealth of cultural traditions along the river or to be mesmerized by its great natural beauty, the sparkle of its waters, the rush of its mountain rapids, the wheel of a soaring redtail or the tranquility of a shad fisherman, riding easy on his oars, waiting to begin work in the slow current quiet of an early spring morning.

— JOHN MYLOD
Executive Director, The Clearwater, Inc.

Grass tussocks line the banks of Silver Mine Lake, Harriman State Park
Overleaf: Bear Mountain Bridge crosses the Hudson River at Anthony's Nose

CARR CLIFTON
PREFACE

Between 1986 and 1988 I traveled the Hudson River watershed in search of remnants of a pristine natural landscape. I traveled alone and lived out of my pickup, which serves as both photography headquarters and home when I am on the road.

I spent the days exploring the trails and roadways that weave through the hills and mountains of the Hudson River Valley, eyes tuned for the vistas, great and small, where I could expose unmarred images of the natural landscape. Nights I studied maps inside my camper, planned the next day's explorations, loaded sheet film and tried to sleep. Dawn found me following the riverside with 50 pounds of camera equipment in tow or, after dodging commuter traffic, draping myself in a black focusing cloth and bending over my view camera on some bridge or busy highway. There I'd wait for morning light to illuminate rock, forest or water.

Many generations ago, my great-, great-, great-, great-, great-grandfather crossed the Atlantic and sailed up the Hudson in search of land where farm and family could prosper. He settled in the shadow of the Adirondacks, and generations of McIntyres and Culberts called the Hudson home. But son by son and daughter by daughter the family moved west in search of wide-open spaces and western opportunity, until what had been a family of farmers became a family of ranchers. I grew up feeling as western as the horizon around me, knowing little of my eastern ancestors or the land they called home.

My trips from west to east became not only photographic explorations of the Hudson River Valley, but journeys back in time to the home of my ancestors. I wanted to retrace my grandfathers' footsteps along the Hudson. I wanted to see an "older" America and find out how the natural landscape was faring after 200 years of intense human exploitation. I also wanted to expose on film some reminders of that first American landscape, which had swelled the imagination of a young and ambitious nation and had inspired, for many, a longing for wildness.

Photographing the Hudson turned out to be the most challenging assignment I have ever accomplished. I'm comfortable with my camera when hiking in grizzly habitat, exposing a lightning storm at 12,000 feet or catching the glint of light off ice fields as my toes and camera shutters freeze in sub-zero weather. I'm content and secure wherever it feels most wild. But while the Hudson has been a "cradle of civilization" for America, nourishing a history and a culture that make most other parts of the country seem provincial in contrast, the stress of human impact on the river's environment has degraded the landscape once considered a hallmark of America.

Despite the Hudson's scenic views and the bucolic quality of its landscapes, I found it difficult, in some places impossible, and often disheartening to find, isolate and frame the pristine, uncompromised images of the natural environment that I look for to photograph. Roads, railroad tracks, jet streams in the sky, power lines and garbage so often got in the way of my intended photographs that, more often than not, I had to abandon large panoramic exposures for mid-range photographs, which focus more on detail than on breadth of place. Sometimes I had to "photo-prep" by removing garbage that lay within the frame of the image I wanted to expose.

The photographs in this book must not be viewed as literal representations of a "real" Hudson landscape, but rather as a collection of images I was able to isolate from the greater context of a scenic but environmentally endangered landscape. These photographs don't describe a place so much as they expose an order of texture, color, pattern and form I encountered in the Hudson River watershed. I photograph in this way not so much to tell the "truth" about a landscape, as to encounter, in the process of photographing, the natural world which inspires and sustains me.

Lichen-encrusted rock ledges in the Shawangunk Mountains, Minnewaska State Park

It's best to remember when viewing a collection of photographs like these that for every beautiful image there's its "shadow." While I do my professional work with a large format 4x5 view camera, I've also begun carrying a 35mm camera to compile another collection of photographs I'm calling "just-outside-the-frame." These images show another "truth" about the American landscape. They show the toll of human negligence, laziness, ignorance and greed: conifer forests killed by acid rain, dead and discolored rivers and streams, shorelines laced with human waste, and garbage strewing the woods like autumn leaves. Sometimes I find myself thinking more about the garbage than I do about photography, for while I seek out the positive and the life-sustaining, more and more I find the other — a degraded, polluted and violated landscape where our man-made poisons collect and threaten the fabric of the earth we share and call home.

The preservation of wildness is the preservation of hope. That's why I'm concerned, in photography, not so much with the beautiful or the scenic as with the wild. It is the feeling in the presence of wildness, so hard to describe in words to those who don't already know it, that gets me up before dawn and inspires me. But all over the world that feeling of wildness is fading like the last light of day and wearing as thin as the ozone.

Sometimes, disheartening though it was, I photographed the Hudson without such inspiration. Then I had to rely on craftsmanship — skill and technique alone. While those photographs may work compositionally, to me they don't "breathe." They don't sing.

Along the Hudson I focused my lens on more man-made objects than I had in the past, on bridges, mansions and pillars, finally making my way to the steel and many-windowed cliffs of Manhattan.

But I wasn't there long. I hurried back to the source, the still-wild peaks of the Adirondacks. I climbed to the top of Mount Marcy and saw ridge after ridge of blue mountains. Rime ice covered the grasses. I followed the melting snow and springs down to Lake Tear of the Clouds, then down Feldspar Brook to the Opalescent River, to the Flowed Land and into Calamity Brook, which flows into the Hudson at the abandoned settlement of Tahawus.

I wandered up and down both sides of the river, crossing every bridge, seeking out waterfalls and tributaries. I explored the Catskills, the mystery mountains, and admired the farms, the history and the homes there.

I followed the cliffs and the rock ledges of the Shawangunk Mountains, where I saw the red brilliance of blueberry and huckleberry bushes in fall and black bear tracks in winter snow. The Shawangunks are delicate and gardenlike, as if everything was carefully placed there by hand. From the high, flat ridges, the river and the valley below seem to be made of golden light.

I like to think that my great-, great-, great-, great-, great-grandfather would recognize some of what I have seen and photographed along the Hudson if he, like Rip Van Winkle, were to wake and return years later. The towns have grown and changed, and most of the forest wilderness is gone. But surely he knew the golden maple leaves drifting on dark water and the red columbine growing from the cracks of rocks in spring. The river and its valley have changed, but some of the images I offer here have spanned time.

People I met along the Hudson love "their" river and take pride in their many successful efforts to restore it. For their love and their successes there is great cause for hope. And with hope comes the possibility of renewing not only the river, but the entire Hudson River watershed.

— CARR CLIFTON

Spring forest and railroad tracks parallel the Hudson River, north of Bear Mountain Bridge

Look Close, Look Far...

Grasses on Algonquin Peak, Adirondack Park and Preserve
Above: Blue violets, Hudson River Valley

"The clock indicates the moment — but what does eternity
         indicate?
We have thus far exhausted trillions of winters and
         summers,
There are trillions ahead, and trillions ahead of them."
— Walt Whitman, "Song of Myself"

Last leaves of autumn on barren sugar maple, Catskill Mountains Park and Preserve

"A few quadrillions of eras, a few octillions of cubic leagues,
do not hazard the span or make it impatient,
They are but parts, anything is but a part.
See ever so far, there is limitless space outside of that,
Count ever so much, there is limitless time around that."
— Walt Whitman, "Song of Myself"

Maple leaves and birch boles along the Opalescent River, Adirondack Park and Preserve

"The groves were God's first temples. Ere man learned
To hew the shaft, and lay the architrave,
And spread the roof above them, — ere he framed
The lofty vault, to gather and roll back
The sound of anthems; in the darkling wood,
Amidst the cool and silence, he knelt down
And offered . . . solemn thanks
And supplication. . . .

Early snowstorm in the Adirondack Mountains, Adirondack Park and Preserve

. . . For his simple heart
Might not resist the sacred influences,
Which, from the stilly twilight of the place,
And from the gray old trunks that high in heaven
Mingled their mossy boughs, and from the sound
Of the invisible breath that swayed at once
All their green tops, stole over him, and bowed
His spirit with the thought of boundless power
And inaccessible majesty."

— William Cullen Bryant, "Forest Hymn"

Hardwood forest in autumn hues thrives near the headwaters of the Hudson River, Adirondack Park and Preserve

"I believe a leaf of grass is no less
        than the journey-work of the stars,
And the pismire is equally perfect, and a
        grain of sand, and the egg of the wren,
And the tree-toad is a chef-d'oeuvre
        for the highest,
And the running blackberry
        would adorn the parlors of heaven,

And the narrowest hinge in my hand
        puts to scorn all machinery,
And the cow crunching with
        depress'd head surpasses any statue,
And a mouse is miracle enough
        to stagger sextillions of infidels. . . . "

— Walt Whitman, "Song of Myself"

The distant profile of Shawangunk Ridge, Shawangunk Mountains

"Nestled at his root
   Is beauty, such as blooms not in the glare
   Of the broad sun. That delicate forest flower,
   With scented breath, and look so like a smile,
   Seems, as it issues from the shapeless mould
   An emanation of the indwelling Life,
   A visible token of the upholding Love,
   That are the soul of this wide universe. . . .

Purple trillium emerges from a bed of fallen leaves along the Hudson River, Washington County

. . . My heart is awed within me, when I think
Of the great miracle that still goes on,
In silence, round me — the perpetual work
Of thy creation, finished, yet renewed
Forever. Written on thy works I read
The lessons of thy own eternity."

— William Cullen Bryant, "Forest Hymn"

Maple sapling, Catskill Mountains Park and Preserve

"What I enjoy is commensurate with the earth and sky itself. It clings to the rocks and trees; it is kindred to the roughness and savagery; it rises from every tangle and chasm; it perches on the dry oak stubs with the hawks and buzzards; . . .

Lake Colden and the Flowed Land as seen from the summit of Algonquin Peak, Adirondack Park and Preserve

". . . the crows shed it from their wings and weave it into their nests of coarse sticks; the fox barks it, the cattle low it, and every mountain path leads to its haunts. I am not a spectator of, but a participator in it. It is not an adornment; its roots strike to the centre of the earth." — *John Burroughs' America*

Forest and cattails, Iona Island Bird Sanctuary

"I hear you whispering there O stars of heaven,
    O suns — O grass of graves — O perpetual transfers
        and promotions. . . .
    Of the turbid pool that lies in the autumn forest,
    Of the moon that descends the steeps of the
        soughing twilight,
    Toss, sparkles of day and dusk — toss on the black stems
        that decay in the muck,
    Toss to the moaning gibberish of the dry limbs."
    — Walt Whitman, "Song of Myself"

Snow and icicles cling to a limb, Catskill Mountains

"I see something of God each hour of the twenty-four,
        and each moment then, . . .
I find letters from God dropt in the street, and every one
        is signed by God's name,
And I leave them where they are, for I know that
        wheresoe'er I go,
Others will punctually come for ever and ever."
— Walt Whitman, "Song of Myself"

Hoarfrost on Bash Bish Creek, Taconic State Park

"The most precious things of life are near at hand, without money and without price. Each of you has the whole wealth of the universe at your very door. All that I ever had, and still have, may be yours by stretching forth your hand and taking it . . . the student and lover of nature has this advantage over people who gad up and down the world seeking some novelty or excitement: he has only to stay at home and see the procession pass. The great globe swings around to him like a revolving showcase; the change of the seasons is like the passage of strange and new countries; the zones of the earth, with all their beauties and marvels, pass one's door and linger long in the passing."

— *John Burroughs' America*

Birch tree and autumn forest along shore of Clear Pond, Adirondack Park and Preserve

"I sit here amid the junipers of the Hudson.... Sometimes a rabbit or a jay or a little warbler brings the woods to my door. A loon on the river, and the Canada lakes are here; the sea gulls and the fish hawk bring the sea; the call of the wild gander at night, what does it suggest? and the eagle flapping by, or floating along on a raft of ice? . . ."

— *John Burroughs' America*

Gertrudes Nose and the Hudson River Valley, Minnewaska State Park

"...when I go to the woods or fields or ascend to the hilltop, I do not seem to be gazing upon beauty at all, but to be breathing it like the air." — *John Burroughs' America*

Autumn in Ulster County, Hudson River Valley

View of the Hudson River south from Breakneck Ridge, Hudson Highlands State Park

From
the
Watershed...

Rime-iced grasses on the summit of Mount Marcy, Adirondack Park
and Preserve   Above: Autumn leaves suspended on pond, Catskill
Mountains Park and Preserve

"The finishing touch is given by the moss with which the rock is everywhere carpeted. Even in the narrow grooves or channels where the water runs the swiftest, the green lining is unbroken. It sweeps down under the stream and up again on the other side, like some firmly woven texture."

— *John Burroughs' America*

Falls on Stony Creek, Catskill Mountains Park and Preserve

Ice along the banks of Lake Tear of the Clouds, Adirondack Mountains

"Lo! all grow old and die — but see, again,
How on the faltering footsteps of decay
Youth presses — ever gay and beautiful youth
In all its beautiful forms. These lofty trees
Wave not less proudly that their ancestors
Moulder beneath them."   —William Cullen Bryant, "Forest Hymn"

Early snowfall on snag and huckleberry bushes in the Shawangunk Mountains, Minnewaska State Park

Snow lines the banks of an icy brook in Frost Valley, Catskill Mountains Park and Preserve

" 'Ay! there are the falls on two sides of us, and the river above and below. . . . sometimes it leaps, sometimes it tumbles; there, it skips; here, it shoots; in one place 'tis white as snow, and in another 'tis green as grass; hereabouts, it pitches into deep hollows, that rumble and quake the 'arth; and hereaway, it ripples and sings like a brook, fashioning whirlpools and gulleys in the old stone, as if't was no harder than trodden clay. . . . First it runs smoothly, as if meaning to go down the descent as things were ordered; then it angles about and faces the shores; nor are there places wanting where it looks backward, as if unwilling to leave the wilderness, to mingle with the salt! Ay, lady, the fine cobweb-looking cloth you wear at your throat, is coarse, and like a fish-net, to little spots I can show you, where the river fabricates all sorts of images, as if, having broke loose from order, it would try its hand at everything. And yet what does it amount to! After the water has been suffered to have its will, for a time, like a headstrong man, it is gathered together by the hand that made it, and a few rods below you may see it all, flowing on steadily towards the sea, as was foreordained from the first foundation of the 'arth!' "

— James Fenimore Cooper, *The Last of the Mohicans*

Kaaterskill Falls, Catskill Mountains Park and Preserve

"He who marvels at the beauty of the world in summer
will find equal cause for wonder and admiration in winter. It
is true the pomp and the pageantry are swept away, but the
essential elements remain — the day and the night, the
mountain and the valley, the elemental play and succession
and the perpetual presence of the infinite sky."

— *John Burroughs' America*

Millbrook Ridge as seen from Trapps Ridge in the Mohonk Preserve, Shawangunk Mountains

Cattails in a Hudson River tidal marsh, Iona Island Bird Sanctuary

"How welcome the smell of [spring], warmed by the sun; the first breath of the reviving earth. How welcome the full, sparkling watercourses, too, everywhere drawing the eye; by and by they will be veiled by the verdure and shrunken by the heat." — *John Burroughs' America*

Bash Bish Creek, Taconic State Park

Spring grass tussocks, Harriman State Park

"To attempt to manufacture beauty is as vain as to attempt to manufacture truth; and to give it to us in poems or any form of art, without a lion of some sort, a lion of truth or fitness or power, is to emasculate it and destroy its volition.

But current poetry is, for the most part, an attempt to do this very thing, to give us beauty without beauty's antecedents and foil. The poets want to spare us the annoyance of the beast. Since beauty is the chief attraction, why not have this part alone, pure and unadulterated — why not pluck the plumage from the bird, the flower from its stalk, the moss from the rock, the shell from the shore, the honey bag from the bee, and thus have in brief what pleases us? Hence, with rare exceptions, one feels, on opening the latest book of poems, like exclaiming, 'Well, here is the beautiful at last divested of everything else — of truth, of power, of utility — and one may add of beauty, too. It charms as color, or flowers, or jewels, or perfume, charms — and that is the end of it.' " — *John Burroughs' America*

Late autumn brings a dusting of snow to Lake Tear of the Clouds high up in the Adirondack Mountains, Adirondack Park and Preserve

"Now [the stream] comes silently along on the top of the rock, spread out and flowing over that thick, dark green moss that is found only in the coldest streams; then drawn into a narrow canal only four or five feet wide, through which it shoots, black and rigid, to be presently caught in a deep basin with shelving, overhanging rocks. . . ." —*John Burroughs' America*

Autumn along the Hudson River near the towns of Hadley and Lake Luzerne, Adirondack Park and Preserve

Tomkins Falls on Barkaboom Stream, Catskill Mountains Park and Preserve

"What a multitude of sins this unstinted charity of the snow covers! How it flatters the ground! . . . It is like some conjurer's trick. The very trees have turned to snow. The smallest branch is like a cluster of great white antlers."

— *John Burroughs' America*

Last autumn leaves along Feldspar Brook, Adirondack Park and Preserve

False hellebore along a feeder stream, Catskill Mountains Park and Preserve

Early morning in the Shawangunk
Mountains, Minnewaska State Park

Into the Valley...

Yonkers and New York City from across the Hudson River at the Palisades   Above: Tidal marsh along the Hudson River, Tivoli Bays Unique Area

"Flood-tide below me! I see you face to face!
Clouds of the west — sun there half an
        hour high — I see you also face to face. . . .

Flow on, river! flow with the flood-tide,
        and ebb with the ebb-tide!
Frolic on, crested and scallop-edg'd waves!
Gorgeous clouds of the sunset! drench with
        your splendor me, or the
        men and women generations after me!"
— Walt Whitman, "Crossing Brooklyn Ferry"

Lone columbine on an outcrop above the Hudson River,
Mills/Norrie State Park   Above: Sunset on the Hudson River
near Athol, Adirondack Park and Preserve

"After a hundred years have
        slept above us
Autumn will still be painting
        the Berkshires;
Gold and purple storms will still
Climb over the Catskills.
They will have to look a long time
For my name in the musty
        corners of libraries;
Utter forgetfulness will mock
Your uncertain ambitions.
But there will be other lovers,
Walking along the hill crests,
Climbing to sit entranced
On pinnacles in the sunset,
In the moonrise.
The Catskills,
The Berkshires,
Have good memories."

— Kenneth Rexroth, "The Thin Edge of Your Pride"

The Hudson River from Cruger Island, Tivoli Bays Unique Area

"The Hudson is a long arm of the sea, and it has something of the sea's austerity and grandeur. I think one might spend a lifetime upon its banks without feeling any sense of ownership in it or becoming at all intimate with it: it keeps one at arm's length." *— John Burroughs' America*

Sunset on the Hudson River, Mills/Norrie State Park
Above: Birch tree and the Hudson River at Cruger Island, Tivoli Bays Unique Area

"The river never seems so much a thing of life as in the spring when it first slips off its icy fetters. The dead comes to life before one's very eyes. The rigid, pallid river is resurrected in a twinkling. You look out of your window one moment, and there is that great, white, motionless expanse; you look again, and there in its place is the tender, dimpling, sparkling water." — *John Burroughs' America*

Dusk along the Hudson River, Putnam County   Above: Shadbush blooms along the Hudson River at Cruger Island, Tivoli Bays Unique Area

"Soft and pale is the moony beam,
Moveless still the glassy stream,
The wave is clear,
        the beach is bright
    With snowy shells and
        sparkling stones;
The shore-surge comes in ripples light,
    In murmurings faint
        and distant moans;
And ever afar in the silence deep
Is heard the splash of the
        sturgeon's leap,
And the bend of his graceful
        bow is seen —
A glittering arch of silver sheen,
Spanning the wave of burnished blue,
And dripping with gems of
        the river dew."

— Joseph Rodman Drake, "The Culprit Fay"

Evening light on the Hudson River, Croton Point

"A child said What is the grass?
      fetching it to me with full hands;
How could I answer the child?
      I do not know what it is any more than he.
I guess it must be the flag of my disposition,
      out of hopeful green stuff woven. . . .
Or I guess the grass is itself a child,
      the produced babe of the vegetation.
Or I guess it is a uniform hieroglyphic,
And it means, Sprouting alike in broad
      zones and narrow zones,
Growing among black folks as among white,
Kanuck, Tuckahoe, Congressman, Cuff. . . ."

— Walt Whitman, "Song of Myself"

Marsh grasses along the Hudson River, Hook Mountain State Park
Above: Evening glow on the Hudson River, Vanderbilt Mansion
National Historic Site

Sunrise on the Hudson River, south of Bear
Mountain

Man
and
the
River...

Dock pilings at sunset on the Hudson River, Hook Mountain State Park
Above: The Vanderbilt Mansion, built in 1898 by Frederick Vanderbilt,
Vanderbilt Mansion National Historic Site, Hyde Park

"One's own landscape comes in time to be a sort of outlying part of himself; he has sowed himself broadcast upon it, and it reflects his own moods and feelings; he is sensitive to the verge of the horizon: cut those trees, and he bleeds; mar those hills, and he suffers." — *John Burroughs' America*

Last light of day shines on the Hudson River, Bear Mountain Bridge

Ranch in spring, south of Germantown

"Then the charm and significance of a day are so subtle and fleeting! Before we know it, it is gone past all recovery. I find that each spring, each summer and fall and winter of my life, has a hue and quality of its own, given by some prevailing mood, a train of thought, an event . . .

Piled firewood at the Van Cortlandt Manor House, a 17th-century Dutch estate, Croton-on-Hudson

". . . an experience — a color or quality of which I am quite unconscious at the time, being too near to it and too completely enveloped by it. But afterward some mood or circumstance, an odor, or fragment of a tune, brings it back as by a flash. . . ." *John Burroughs' America*

The Ardsley House, Catskill Mountains Park and Preserve

"But in natural history there is no need to counterfeit the truth; the reality always suffices, if you have eyes to see it and ears to hear it. . . . a race that . . . fears the touch of the soil, that has no footpaths, no community of ownership in the land which they imply, that warns off the walker as a trespasser, that knows no way but the highway, the carriage way, that forgets the stile, the footbridge, that even ignores the rights of the pedestrian in the public road, providing no escape for him but in the ditch or up the bank, is in a fair way to a far more serious degeneracy."

— *John Burroughs' America*

Bridge spanning the Hudson River near Athol and Warrensburg, Adirondack Park and Preserve

"I too am not a bit tamed, I too am untranslatable,
I sound my barbaric yawp over the roofs of the world. . . .
I depart as air, I shake my white locks at the runaway sun,
I effuse my flesh in eddies, and drift it in lacy jags.
I bequeath myself to the dirt to grow from the grass I love,
If you want me again look for me under your boot-soles."
— Walt Whitman, "Song of Myself"

Memorial to John Sedgwick, commander of the 6th Army Corps, who was killed in battle during the Civil War, West Point Military Academy

Detail of European marble sculpture at the Vanderbilt Mansion, a 54-room Italian Renaissance masterpiece, Vanderbilt Mansion National Historic Site

81

"That I walk up my stoop, I pause to consider if it really be,
A morning-glory at my window satisfies me more than
the metaphysics of books.
To behold the day-break!
The little light fades the immense and
diaphanous shadows,
The air tastes good to my palate.
Hefts of the moving world at innocent gambols silently
rising, freshly exuding . . .

Clermont on the Hudson River, home to Robert Livingston, co-inventor of the first steamboat in 1807, Clermont State Historic Park

. . . Scooting obliquely high and low.
    Something I cannot see puts upward libidinous prongs,
    Seas of bright juice suffuse heaven.
    The earth by the sky staid with, the daily close of
       their junction,
    The heav'd challenge from the east that moment
       over my head,
    The mocking taunt, See then whether you shall be master!"
    — Walt Whitman, "Song of Myself"

Mills Mansion, a turn-of-the-century retreat designed by architect Stanford White for Ogden Mills, Mills Mansion
State Historic Site

"The perception of cosmical beauty comes by a vital original process. It is in some measure a creative act, and those works that rest upon it make demands — perhaps extraordinary ones — upon the reader or beholder. We regard mere surface glitter, or mere verbal sweetness, in a mood entirely passive and with a pleasure entirely profitless. The beauty of excellent stage scenery seems much more obvious and easy of apprehension than the beauty of trees and hills themselves, inasmuch as the act of association in the mind is much easier and cheaper than the act of original perception."

— *John Burroughs' America*

Barn in Keene Valley, Adirondack Park and Preserve

85

"And I know that the hand of God is the promise
        of my own,
And I know that the spirit of God is the brother
        of my own . . .
And that a kelson of the creation is love,
And limitless are leaves stiff or drooping
        in the fields,
And brown ants in the little wells
        beneath them,
And mossy scabs of the worm fence, heap'd
        stones, elder, mullein and poke-weed."
— Walt Whitman, "Song of Myself"

Miller's quarters at Philipsburg Manor, Upper Mills, a grist mill
complex established by Frederick Philipse, circa 1682, North
Tarrytown   Above: Philipsburg Manor, near the mouth of the
Pocantico River, North Tarrytown

"The youth of the earth is in the soil and in the trees and verdure that spring from it; its age is in the rocks; in the great stone book of the geologic strata its history is written. Even if we do not know our geology, there is something in the face of a cliff and in the look of a granite boulder that gives us pause. . . ." — *John Burroughs' America*

Mohonk Mountain House, last of the great 19th-century Hudson River Valley resort hotels, Shawangunk Mountains

"Rocks do not recommend the land to the tiller of the soil,
but they recommend it to those who reap a harvest of another
sort — the artist, the poet, the walker, the student and lover
of all primitive open-air things."   — *John Burroughs' America*

French Huguenot House, circa 1692, resides on "the oldest street in America with its original houses," New Paltz

Mills Mansion overlooks the Hudson River,
Mills Mansion State Historic Site

Images
of
Wildness...

Balsam fir covered in snow, Adirondack Park and Preserve
Above: Fog on Trapps Ridge, Shawangunk Mountains

"Stranger, if thou hast learned
                    a truth which needs
No school of long experience,
                    that the world
Is full of guilt and misery,
                    and hast seen
Enough of all its sorrows,
                    crimes, and cares,
To tire thee of it, enter this wild wood
And views the haunts of Nature.
                    The calm shade
Shall bring a kindred calm,
                    and the sweet breeze
That makes the green leaves dance,
                    shall waft a balm
To thy sick heart.
                    Thou wilt find nothing here
Of all that pained thee
                    in the haunts of men
And made thee loathe thy life."

— William Cullen Bryant, "Inscription for the Entrance to a Wood"

Fall-colored huckleberry shoots invade a rock fissure in the
Shawangunk Mountains, Minnewaska State Park

"There is a glow about this flower as if color emanated from it as from a live coal. The eye is baffled and does not seem to reach the surface of the petal; it does not see the texture or material part as it does in other flowers, but rests in a steady, still radiance." — *John Burroughs' America*

Serviceberry blossoms in spring, Albany County

Flowering dogwood, Harriman State Park

"The smallest sprout shows there is really no death,
And if ever there was it led forward life, and does not wait
    at the end to arrest it,
And ceas'd the moment life appear'd.
All goes onward and outward, nothing collapses,
And to die is different from what any one supposed,
    and luckier."   — Walt Whitman, "Song of Myself"

Early snowfall on a brook near the town of North Hudson, Adirondack Park and Preserve

Ice forms on the Opalescent River, Adirondack Park and Preserve

"The time of the falling of leaves has come again. Once more in our morning walk we tread upon carpets of gold and crimson, of brown and bronze, woven by the winds or the rains out of these delicate textures while we slept. How beautifully the leaves grow old! How full of light and color are their last days! . . . Both the pine and the hemlock make friends with the birch, the maple, and the oak, and one of the most pleasing and striking features of our autumnal scenery is a mountainside sown broadcast with these intermingled trees, forming a combination of colors like the richest tapestry, the dark green giving body and permanence, the orange and yellow giving light and brilliancy." — *John Burroughs' America*

Birch trunks in an autumn forest, headwaters of the Hudson River, Adirondack Park and Preserve

"From an opening between the trees he could overlook all the lower country for many a mile of rich woodland. He saw at a distance the lordly Hudson, far, far below him, moving on its silent but majestic course . . . and at last losing itself in the blue highlands." — Washington Irving, "Rip Van Winkle"

Eastern white pine near Elk Lake, Adirondack Park and Preserve

Tree roots along the banks of the Hudson River, Mills/Norrie State Park

"To me, nothing else about a tree is so remarkable as the extreme delicacy of the mechanisms by which it grows and lives. . . . So it looks as though the tree was almost made of matter and spirit, like man; the ether with its vibrations, on the one hand, and the earth with its inorganic compounds, on the other. . . ." — *John Burroughs' America*

Fall reflection and leaves on pond, Adirondack Mountains

Awosting Falls in the Shawangunk Mountains, Minnewaska State Park

Oaks in autumn forest, Shawangunk
Mountains

"There was never any more inception than there is now,
Nor any more youth or age than there is now,
And will never be any more perfection than there is now,
Nor any more heaven or hell than there is now.
Urge and urge and urge,
Always the procreant urge of the world."
— Walt Whitman, "Song of Myself"

Cattails and maple, near New Paltz

Shelf fungi and moss-covered log, near Rockland Lake in the Palisades

"Smile O voluptuous cool-breath'd earth!
    Earth of the slumbering and liquid trees!
    Earth of departed sunset — earth of the mountains
        misty-topt!
    Earth of the vitreous pour of the full moon just tinged
        with blue!
    Earth of shine and dark . . ."
    — Walt Whitman, "Song of Myself"

The Hudson River near the towns of Hadley and Lake Luzerne, Adirondack Park and Preserve

Lichen patterns on glaciated rock ledges, Shawangunk Mountains, Minnewaska State Park

Technical Information

The images within this book were primarily made using a Toyo 4x5 field view camera. Lenses of 90mm, 135mm, 180mm, 240mm and 360mm focal lengths were used. Fujichrome 50 and 100 and Ektachrome 64 were used exclusively with the large format. Three images within this book were made with an Olympus OM-1 35mm camera on Kodachrome 64.

Exposures were calculated with a Gossen Luna-Pro meter for incident light readings and a Pentax spot meter for reflected light readings using both a gray card and values of light in the landscape. Apertures varied from f/8 to f/64. Shutter speeds ranged from 1/60 of a second to 10 seconds.

Acknowledgements

I would like to thank Hitachi America, Ltd. for their generous support. Without their help, the production of this book would not have been possible. I would also like to thank Hardie and Marcie Truesdale of New Paltz, New York, for their many sailing trips on the Hudson and for providing a roof over my head when I became weary.

— C.C.